Praying *in* color

Kids' Edition

Sybil MacBeth

PARACLETE PRESS
BREWSTER, MASSACHUSETTS

Many thanks to Jane Heill, Allie Burton, Andy MacBeth, Lisa DiScenza, Lynn Hunter, and Page Zyromski for their ideas and suggestions about the manuscript. Thanks also to Kathy Carmean for coining the phrase "parking lot for distractions."

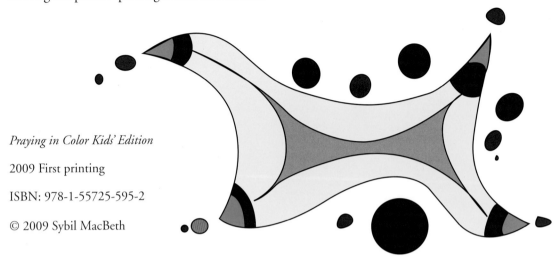

Praying in Color Kids' Edition

2009 First printing

ISBN: 978-1-55725-595-2

© 2009 Sybil MacBeth

Unless otherwise indicated, all Scripture quotations are from the New Revised Standard Version Bible, copyright © 1989 by the Division of Education of the National Council of Churches of Christ in the U.S.A., and are used by permission. All rights reserved.

Scripture quotations designated KJV are from the Authorized King James Version of the Bible.

Library of Congress Cataloging-in-Publication Data

MacBeth, Sybil.
  Praying in color / Sybil MacBeth. -- Kids' ed.
     p. cm.
  ISBN 978-1-55725-595-2
  1. Prayer--Christianity--Juvenile literature. 2. Color drawing--Religious aspects--Christianity--Juvenile literature. I. Title.
  BV212.M33 2009
  248.3'2--dc22
                        2008045025

10 9 8 7 6 5 4 3 2 1

Published by Paraclete Press
Brewster, Massachusetts
www.paracletepress.com

Printed in China

Prayer Problems

If you have had one or more of these prayer problems, you are not alone. Join the frustrated pray-ers club!

You feel antsy and fidgety when you try to be still and pray.

You start to pray, then fall asleep.

You're tired of the same old prayers you've said since preschool.

You run out of words, but the prayer doesn't feel finished.

You can't wait for your prayer time to be over and done with.

You can't find the words to say what you think or feel.

You wonder whether God is listening or even cares.

You want to like praying, but it just feels like another chore.

You start to pray but realize that you're thinking about tomorrow's soccer game, a friend's sleepover, or homework.

You tell God exactly how you feel and then wonder whether God will be angry.

What is Prayer? 2

Prayer is the way we spend time with God. People often describe prayer as a conversation. Conversation includes both talking and listening. We talk to God and we listen to God in our prayers. When we talk we use WORDS. Here are some of the things we say WITH WORDS in our prayers:

Thank you God for the stars and the trees,
for my family, friends, and teachers, for passing
my science test, for pizza, for Jesus. . . .

Why does my math teacher always call
on Henry in class and never me?

My friend Rachel has something called leukemia.
Help her not to be scared and make her better.

Dear God,
please watch over my mom
when she flies to Chicago today.

Jesus, you are so wonderful
and awesome!

Sometimes I hate my brother.
He's so mean to me.

God,
are you really listening
to me?

I'm sorry I copied off of Josh's paper today.
It was just one question.
But I guess that's still cheating.

Please God,
help me to be a better basketball player
so I can make the fifth-grade team.

4

My mom and dad are getting
a divorce. I'm really sad
and angry. Why can't they
love each other?

This has been the best day.
Thank you, thank you, thank you!

Dear Jesus, help me to be nice
to my little sister even when she
grabs the remote and changes the
channel when I'm watching TV.

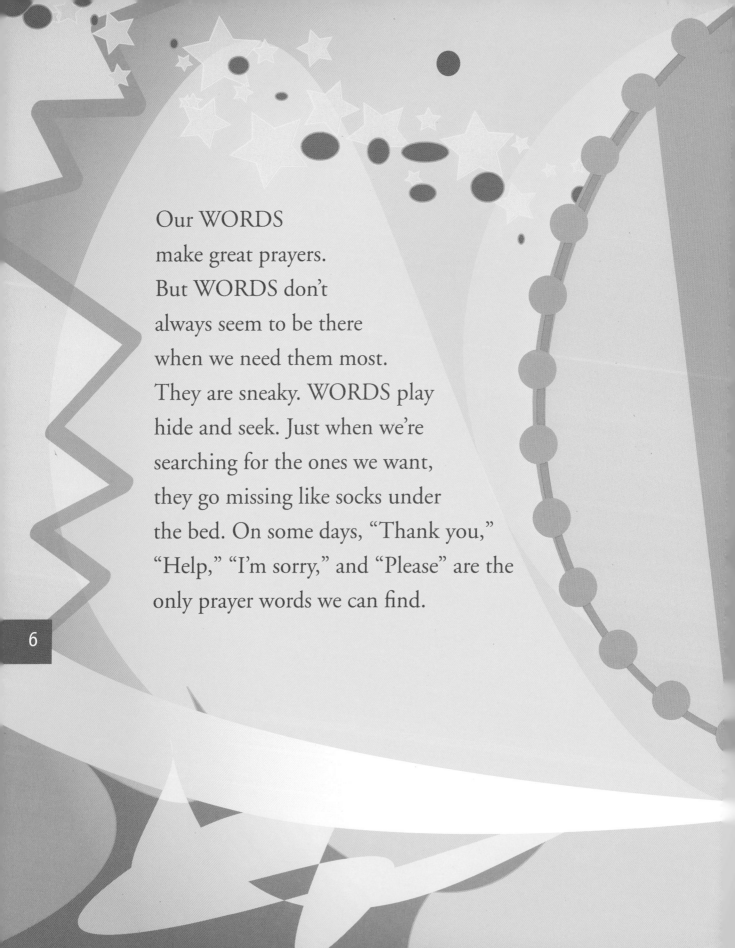

Our WORDS
make great prayers.
But WORDS don't
always seem to be there
when we need them most.
They are sneaky. WORDS play
hide and seek. Just when we're
searching for the ones we want,
they go missing like socks under
the bed. On some days, "Thank you,"
"Help," "I'm sorry," and "Please" are the
only prayer words we can find.

Praying WITHOUT WORDS is another option. But what do you DO, if you're not using words? How do you pray for yourself or other people without words? How do you get quiet and listen to what God might say? Or, as the writer of 1 Kings 19:12 in the Bible might ask, "How do you hear the 'still small voice' or the 'gentle whisper' of God?"

Look at the drawing on the next page. Believe it or not, it is a prayer. It is a prayer doodle for Ben, Keisha, Matt, Ashley, and Taylor.

Ben had his ninth birthday.
Keisha broke her arm.
Matt's grandfather died.
Ashley is going on a trip.
Taylor was in a fight and is grounded.

Ben and Ashley had happy events in their lives. Keisha, Matt, and Taylor had some unhappy events. We pray for people in both happy and unhappy times. We offer our positive and grateful thoughts to God, but also our scared and worried thoughts too.

In the drawing, the pray-er drew a shape with her name for God in the center. She added arcs and color. Then she drew doodles for each friend. As she drew, she pictured each person in the presence and care of God. She used no words. The drawing *was* the prayer.

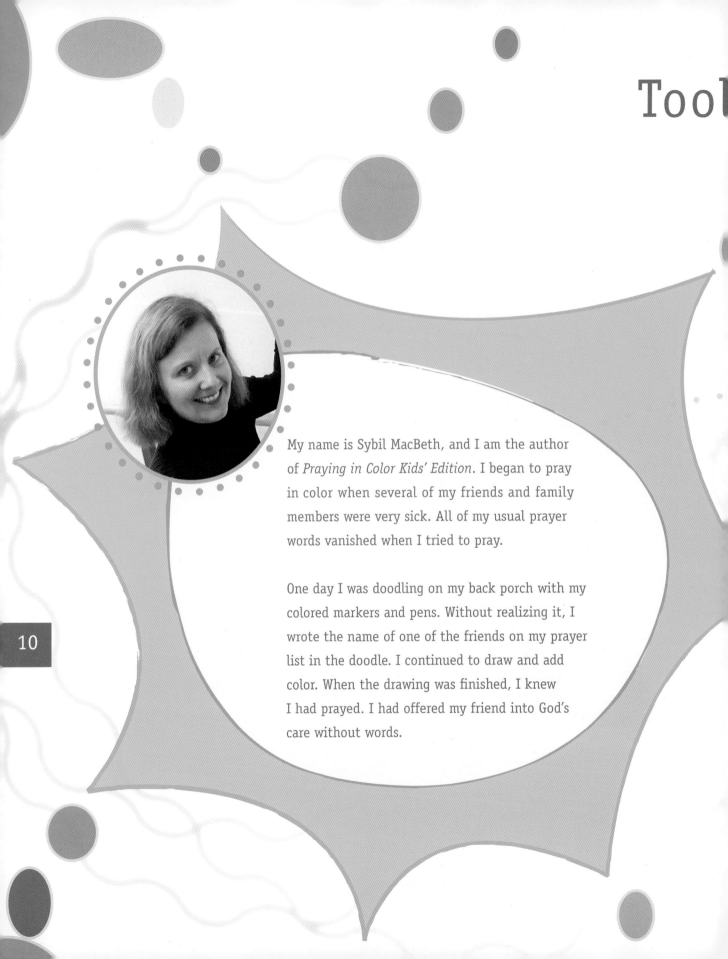

My name is Sybil MacBeth, and I am the author of *Praying in Color Kids' Edition*. I began to pray in color when several of my friends and family members were very sick. All of my usual prayer words vanished when I tried to pray.

One day I was doodling on my back porch with my colored markers and pens. Without realizing it, I wrote the name of one of the friends on my prayer list in the doodle. I continued to draw and add color. When the drawing was finished, I knew I had prayed. I had offered my friend into God's care without words.

Here are some tools you will need for Praying in Color:

1. Doodling Ideas
2. God Names

Doodling Ideas

Doodling is playful, aimless drawing. When the famous artist Paul Klee painted and drew, he said he was "taking a line for a walk." Doodling is like that. Except in doodling, the "line takes us for a walk," kind of like a puppy on a leash. When we doodle, we don't necessarily know where we are going. We don't have an end picture in mind.

To pray in color, you don't need to be an artist. You don't need to be able to draw a cat or a flower or anything at all. You just need to put a pen and colored markers or pencils on a piece of paper and start moving.

Here are some shapes and movements you can make when you doodle:

Draw

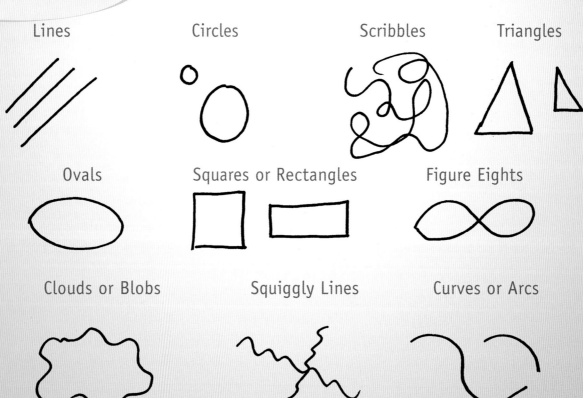

Lines   Circles   Scribbles   Triangles

Ovals   Squares or Rectangles   Figure Eights

Clouds or Blobs   Squiggly Lines   Curves or Arcs

Scallops   Teeth   Polka Dots   Dots

Wacky Shapes   Petals   Spirals   Hearts

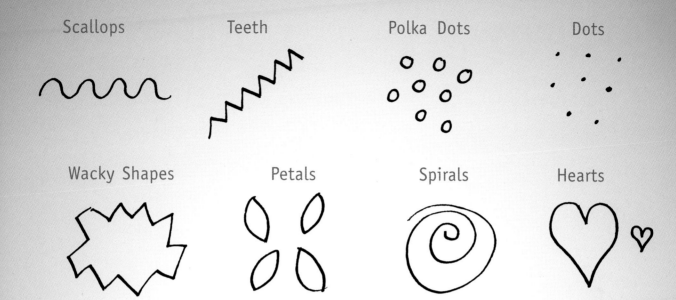

Combine together the ideas above:

Lines with Lines   Rectangles with Arcs   Hearts with Polka Dots

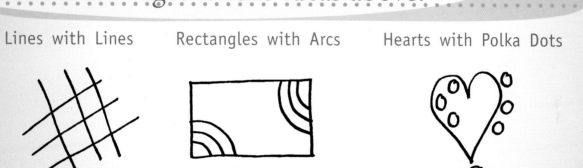

Circles with Triangles   Petals with Scribbles   Teeth with Figure Eights

13

The number of ways to combine different shapes is huge. You can invent new shapes and patterns for yourself. If you like to draw *real* things like trees, crosses, flowers, or boats, go for it. Just don't get hung up in the drawing. The point is to keep your hands busy and your body involved so you can pray.

Beloved On

Lord

Holy Spirit

Abba Father Jesu

Redeemer

God SAVIOR

God Names

When we begin to pray, we often use a name to address God. The Bible gives us many names. People throughout history have used those old names as well as new ones they have learned in their religious traditions. Here are some of the most common names we use when we pray:

Adonai

Father Mother God Yahweh

We can add adjectives to the names above to describe them in a special way.

Almighty God   Loving God   Holy Jesus

Precious Lord   Gracious and Loving God   Divine Spirit

Dearest Savior   Holy One

Your name for God might be different from the ones on this list. That's fine. Try other names to see how they feel when you use them in your prayers.

16

Now grab your drawing supplies—paper, markers, crayons, gel pens—and find a place to pray. You can pray on the couch, in the car, outside, on the floor, in bed, on an airplane, at your desk. . . . In Matthew 6, Jesus tells us: ". . . Whenever you pray, go into your room (or closet) and shut the door. . . ." With a clipboard, magazine, or notebook behind your paper, you can turn any place into a prayer room and shut an imaginary door on the noises of the world.

Getting Started

Begin your prayer time with one of these activities:

try this!!

1

Read a passage from the Bible.
Here are some possibilities:

"This is the day that the LORD has made;
let us rejoice and be glad in it."
Psalm 118:24

"Seek ye first the kingdom of God, and his
righteousness; and all these things shall be added
unto you." Matthew 6:33 KJV

"O come, let us sing to the LORD;
let us make a joyful noise to the rock of our salvation!"
Psalm 95:1

"Be strong and courageous;
do not be frightened or
dismayed, for the LORD your
God is with you wherever
you go." Joshua 1:9

17

Turn the page for more
Bible verses!

1

"Make me to know your ways, O LORD; teach me your paths. Lead me in your truth, and teach me, for you are the God of my salvation; for you I wait all day long."
Psalm 25:4–5

Stretch your arms over your head, reach
for the sky, and shout, "Thank you, God."
Invite your body into prayer with you.

or this!!

2

Take several deep breaths.
Let out a slow, noisy sigh after each one.

"The spirit of God has made me,
and the breath of the Almighty gives me life."
Job 33:4

or this!!

3

If none of these ideas
appeals to you, just pick up your pen
and your markers, and begin to pray in color.

With a black pen, draw a shape on the page—a cloud, a square, a squiggly line, a spiral. . . . Write one of the names for God in the shape or near the shape.

When we write our name for God, we ask God to be present with us in our prayer time.

Another way to start is to leave the first shape empty. We don't always know what name to call God, but we know that God is bigger than any of the names we use. Think of the empty space as a window for you to see God and for God to see you.

If your mind begins to wander, try the following: Say your God name to yourself in silence or out loud. Then take a big breath and exhale. Repeat these steps several times. This is one way to stop distracting thoughts.

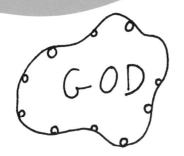

Add detail to the drawing. Use dots, lines, circles, or whatever doodle your hand wants to make. Let your hand take your eye for a walk.

Continue to doodle in and around the shape. Think of each mark of your pen as time you spend with God in prayer.

Keep drawing until the picture feels finished.

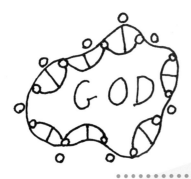

By being quiet, we give God the chance to speak.

What would God speaking to you sound like? It might not even be a sound. A feeling of peace and calm might come over you. A new and important idea might enter your head. A great love for other people might fill you and surround you. Or, you might just hear the sound of your own breath. The Bible sometimes describes God's voice as wind or breath.

Sitting in silence with our attention on God is as powerful as praying with words. When we sit in a room with family or people we love, we don't always speak. We just enjoy being surrounded by their love.

Add color to the picture.

When the God prayer is completed, move to another space on the page. Draw a new shape or design and include the name of a person for whom you want to pray.

Add designs, doodles, and color. Choose colors that will stay in your memory, that you particularly like, or that remind you of the person for whom you pray.

We pray for other people for many reasons:

- We pray because we are happy or grateful for them.
- We pray because we are scared, sad, or confused for them.
- We pray because they are sick or hurt.
- We pray because they hurt our feelings and we are angry with them.
- We pray for our friends and family just because we love them and want to surround them with God's love.
- We pray to place our worry about others into God's hands. The Bible says, "Do not worry about anything, but in everything by prayer and supplication with thanksgiving let your requests be made known to God" (Philippians 4:6).

The Bible also says, ". . . pray for one another, so that you may be healed" (James 5:16). Praying for others is called intercessory prayer. We ask God to heal their bodies, to keep them safe, to make their sadness go away, and to fill them with love.

In intercessory prayer, we can pray for any of God's creatures or creations. We pray for countries, for the world and its leaders, for the earth, or even for pets.

Add another person to your prayer drawing. Repeat the process of drawing and praying. Add detail and color the same way you did with the first person.

Add a new person to the prayer "list."

Add another person to the drawing. Draw with pen and colors until you have created a doodle for all of the people for whom you want to pray.

When you finish praying for a person, say something like, "Amen," "I'll be back," or, "God of Love, see my prayer." Then add another person to the drawing.

If the needs and concerns of a person are very great, take several deep breaths to release any worry that you might carry to the next person. Or stand up for a moment and physically shake away those cares.

Sit with the drawing in front of you. Let the names, images, and colors plant themselves in your brain. Spend another moment with each person in silence. Take your sketchbook or page with you. Carry it in your backpack, put it next to your computer, or stick it on your refrigerator. Find someplace where your eyes will see the drawing during the day.

In this wordless prayer practice, daydreams and distractions will probably enter your mind and beg for your attention. Notice them, but don't talk to them. Keep your focus on the person for whom you pray.

Create a little "parking lot" for your distractions. If you need to finish a school assignment, make your bed, or remember someone's birthday, write a word or two in the parking lot to remind you to deal with it after your prayer time.

To prevent an army of distractions from marching through your head, think about the face or the entire person as if you were sitting with him or her in conversation.

There is no order in which you must complete the drawing and coloring. You can choose to draw the entire prayer chart first, then return and fill in the color. This gives you a second chance to visit the people for whom you pray.

Another way to add to the original drawing is to write words or thoughts next to a person's doodle. After you have spent a day or two praying for a person in silence, words may come to you.

You can include two people in one space—a brother and sister, a mother and father, a couple, grandparents.

Sometimes, the first person who needs your prayer attention is YOU. Don't be afraid to write your own name.

When you have finished praying, do something physical to let go of any worry you have for the people on the page. Stand up and take deep breaths. Shake out your arms and legs. Say a big "Amen" or "Thank you, God."

Your colorful prayers may pop up in your mind throughout the day. They are a reminder that you have given these persons into the care of God. Remember, you have chosen not to worry but to pray for them. Picture them in color surrounded by the love and care you offered when you sat and prayed for them.

Keep the drawing for several days as your visual prayer list. Look at it several times each day. Pray for each person in the drawing again. See each one as a beloved child of God. If you want, add doodles for other people.

If you have never doodled before or are unsure how to begin your prayer drawing, you can use some of the ideas on the next few pages to get started.

Trace the shapes on the left on a piece of paper. Write in the names of the people you are praying for. Add color and detail to the shapes as you pray for them.

Draw a squiggly line. Add flags or leaves.

Trace around your hand. Write your God name in the palm. Let each fingertip represent a person. If you have more than 5 people, let a finger hold other names.

Grab a utensil from a kitchen drawer or a tool from your parents' workbench and trace around it to get started.

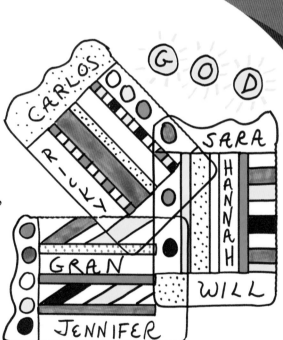

Look at your own hands during the day. Remember who was on each finger in your picture. Pray for each person all over again!

This prayer drawing was started by tracing around a pancake flipper. Stripes, circles, dots, and color were added.

You can trace around cookie cutters, a fork, scissors, or a hammer as a way to get started.

Trace around a dinner plate. Think of this big circle as the
God circle. Inside, trace smaller circles (use glasses or cups)
for each person.

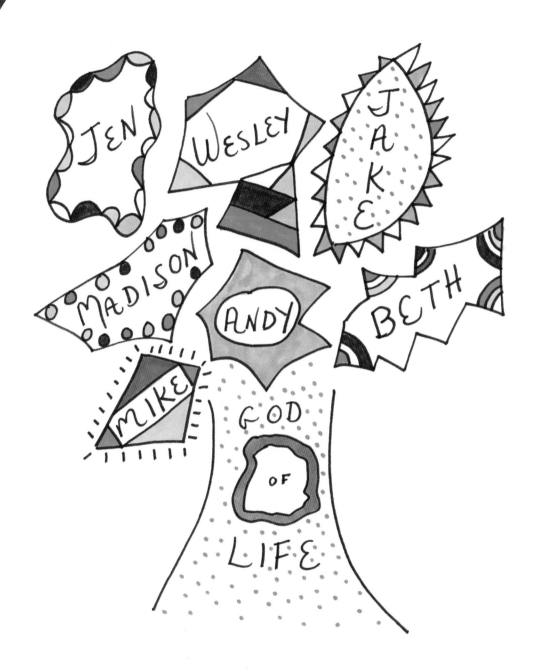

Draw a big tree trunk. Add weird-shaped leaves. Don't worry
if the drawing doesn't look anything like a real tree!

Sunday	Monday	Tuesday	Wednesday	Thursday	Friday	Saturday
			1 AMANDA	2 U S A	3 DONUT	4 PAUL
5 IRAQ	6 MARCUS	7 OUR PRESIDENT	8	9	10	11
12	13	14	15	16	17	18
19	20	21	22	23	24	25
26	27	28	29	30	31	

Create a weekly or monthly calendar on your computer. Or ask your parents if they have an extra calendar to give you. Use the boxes to pray for someone each day.

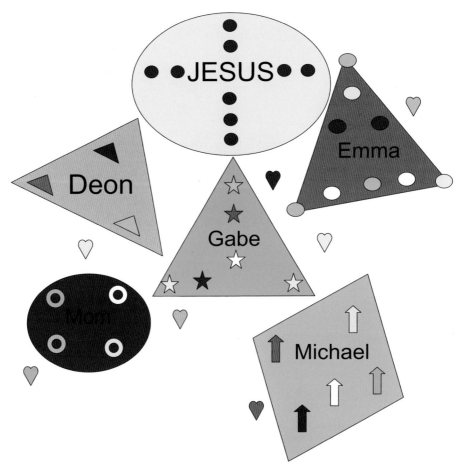

Use a drawing menu or program on your computer to create a variety of shapes. Print out the page and use it to make your prayer drawing. Or try praying on your computer using the shapes, designs, and colors of the drawing program.

You can save or print your drawing, e-mail it to friends who will also pray, or make it your screensaver of the day.

raying in Color Prayers

We often pray for other people. Sometimes we are the people who need the prayers. It's okay to pray for yourself.

Instead of making a separate shape for God, you can circle the entire drawing with your God name or some words from the Bible.

Imagine that you are surrounded by God's love and protection.

When we worship God, we talk about our love and devotion. Draw a praise and worship prayer. This is like a Valentine card to God.

Saying "I love you," or "I worship you" to God is not always easy. We might feel shy or embarrassed. In your Valentine, write names, feelings, or adjectives that come to mind when you think of God.

Sometimes we need to say "I'm sorry" for a bunch of things. Draw a forgiveness or confession prayer.

After you have prayed, ask God what you should do about the things for which you are sorry. Sometimes you might need to apologize. Sometimes telling God what you have done will be enough.

Draw a gratitude or thanksgiving prayer.
Fill the page with the many things for which
you are thankful.

"AND WHAT DOES THE LORD REQUIRE OF YOU BUT TO DO JUSTICE, AND TO LOVE KINDNESS, AND TO WALK HUMBLY WITH YOUR GOD?"

Micah 6:8

Learn and pray a Scripture passage. Take a few words at a time. Draw around them. Say the words over and over again as you draw and memorize. Add more words from the passage and repeat the process.

Draw a stillness prayer.
Write your God name on the page.
Just draw and listen.

Dear God

37

Prayers can be in color or in black and white only. Sometimes color doesn't feel right. Or sometimes you might not have your colored pencils or markers with you. Use just a pen or a pencil to draw.

Remember,
Praying in Color is a way
to pray with your eyes, your
ears, and your hands. It invites your
mind, your heart, and your body into
the prayer. You can use words or you
can be quiet. What matters is that you
want to be closer to God. May peace
and love be with you as you
draw a new path to God.